CENGAGE Learning

Drama for Students, Volume 18

Project Editor: David Galens

Editorial: Anne Marie Hacht, Michelle Kazensky, Ira Mark Milne, Pam Revitzer, Kathy Sauer, Timothy J. Sisler, Jennifer Smith, Carol Ullmann

Research: Michelle Campbell, Tracie Richardson

Permissions: Debra J. Freitas

Manufacturing: Stacy Melson

Imaging and Multimedia: Leitha Etheridge-Sims, Lezlie Light, Dave G. Oblender, Kelly A. Quin, Luke Rademacher

Product Design: Pamela A. E. Galbreath

For more information, contact

Gale
27500 Drake Rd.
Farmington Hills, MI 48331-3535
Or you can visit our Internet site at
http://www.gale.com

guarantee the accuracy of the data contained herein. The Gale Group, Inc. accepts no payment for listing; and inclusion in the publication of any organization, agency, institution, publication, service, or individual does not imply endorsement of the editors or publisher. Errors brought to the attention of the publisher and verified to the satisfaction of the publisher will be corrected in future editions.

ISBN 0-7876-6815-X
ISSN 1094-9232

Printed in the United States of America
10 9 8 7 6 5 4 3 2 1

The Playboy of the Western World

J. M. Synge 1907

Introduction

J(ohn) M(illington) Synge's *The Playboy of the Western World* caused riots during its opening week in Dublin in 1907. Inspired by his close observations of the inhabitants of the Aran Islands off the western coast of Ireland, Synge based the play on a historical incident. His realistic yet poetic depiction of that incident and the manners and mores of Irish life angered many who thought the play indecent and guilty of promoting negative stereotypes. Critical acclaim, however, has grown over the years to the point where it is now regarded as the masterwork of one of the most highly regarded Irish playwrights in the modern age.

The play focuses on the reception given to Christy Mahon as he wanders into a small Irish village, declaring that he has just murdered his father. The villagers initially embrace Christy, determining that his courageous act has made him "the playboy of the western world." Their vision of him, however, soon changes as the plot develops. In his depiction of the interaction between Christy and the villagers, and especially of the relationship between Christy and Pegeen Flaherty, an attractive, strong-willed, young local woman, Synge explores the effects of social conventions and celebrates the power of the imagination.

Author Biography

J. M. Synge was born on April 16, 1871, in the Dublin suburb of Newton Little, to John Hatch and Kathleen Traill Synge. After his father died a year later, Synge, his three brothers, and one sister were raised in a comfortable, upper-class home by their devoutly religious mother. Synge suffered from poor health during his youth, which eventually prompted his mother to have him tutored at home. He began his studies in music theory and Irish history and language at Trinity College in Dublin when he was seventeen and completed a bachelor's degree in 1892. Synge began to write poetry during his years at Trinity as well as at the Royal Irish Academy of Music, where he completed graduate work in music theory.

Synge left Ireland in 1893 to study music in Germany, but his stage fright caused him to reconsider his career choice. A year later, Synge began language and literature studies at the Sorbonne. During his time in Paris, Synge met William Butler Yeats, who would have a dramatic effect on the rest of his life. Yeats inspired Synge to go to the Aran Islands, off the coast of Ireland and, as Yeats notes in his preface to *The Well of the Saints*, encouraged him to "live there as if you were one of the people themselves; express a life that has never found expression." For four years, Synge studied Irish life on the islands as he took photographs of the islanders and careful notes on their speech and habits.

In 1901, he turned his notes into a collection of essays, *The Aran Islands*, and wrote his first play, *When the Moon Has Set*. Two verse plays followed in 1902, but Synge would not develop his mature style until later that year when he penned three plays: *Riders to the Sea*, *In the Shadow of the Glen*, and *The Tinker's Wedding*. On October 8, 1903, *In the Shadow of the Glen* was the first play shown by the Irish National Theatre Society, run by Yeats and Lady Gregory. Though the play initially received a mixed reaction, due to its honest depiction of Irish life, it later gained success during its run in Dublin and England. *Riders to the Sea* earned positive reviews in Ireland and England.

While writing his next play, *The Playboy of the Western World*, Synge became ill with Hodgkin's disease, which delayed the play's opening. *The Playboy of the Western World* became the most controversial production of the Irish National Theatre. Theatergoers rioted during initial performances in response to what they deemed to be a degrading portrait of Irish life. Controversy followed productions of the play for years. However, by the later part of the twentieth century, it came to be recognized as Synge's masterwork.

Synge drafted *Deirdre of the Sorrows* during hospital visits as he battled his increasingly debilitating illness. He died on March 24, 1909, in Dublin without having had time to revise it.

Plot Summary

Act 1

The *Playboy of the Western World* opens in a country public house owned by Michael Flaherty, father to Pegeen, who is preparing for her upcoming wedding to Shawn Keogh, a young farmer. Shawn arrives and is uneasy about being alone with her. Pegeen complains about being left by herself at night, fearing some harm will come to her. They argue about Shawn, who is waiting for the local priest to get a dispensation allowing their marriage, since they are cousins. Pegeen insists that Shawn should be more daring. When her father and local farmers Philly O'Cullen and Jimmy Farrell arrive, they join Pegeen in berating Shawn about his fear of doing anything to displease the Church.

Christy Mahon soon arrives exhausted and frightened, asking whether the police often come to the pub. When Michael assures him that they do not, all begin to quiz him about why he is running from the law. After several wrong guesses, Christy admits that he killed his father. The others embrace him as a courageous young man, and Michael promptly gives him a job helping out Pegeen, which delights his daughter. With the exception of Shawn, who does not appreciate the interest Pegeen is taking in Christy, they all assert that Pegeen will now be safe at night. Pegeen quickly dismisses

Shawn, telling him to seek out the priest.

After Christy tells Pegeen the details of his father's murder, which increases her admiration for him, the Widow Quin arrives full of curiosity about the newcomer. Pegeen and the Widow Quin battle over Christy's attentions until he declares that he will stay in the pub. After the Widow Quin departs, Pegeen declares that she will not be marrying Shawn, and Christy goes to sleep wondering at his good fortune.

Act 2

The next morning four girls from the village, Sara, Susan, Nelly, and Honor, come to see Christy, wanting to meet the man who killed his father. They all offer him presents and admire his brave act. When the Widow Quin arrives, she entreats Christy to tell them all the details of the murder. Christy takes great pleasure in telling the story and afterwards all call him a hero.

When Pegeen arrives, she chases everyone out and angrily orders Christy to work. She tries to scare him away from talking to the village girls by suggesting that they might tell the police. Shawn arrives and tells Pegeen her sheep are in a neighbor's garden, and she runs out. Shawn then tries to convince Christy to accept a passage to America, admitting that he fears Christy will interfere with his plans to marry Pegeen. Christy refuses the ticket but accepts the new clothes Shawn has brought him. The Widow Quin soon convinces the despondent Shawn that she will marry Christy and so clear the way for him with Pegeen.

Just as Christy begins to believe himself to be the hero all claim he is, he spots his father and hides from him. Mahon explains to the Widow Quin that Christy hit him but he recovered. Mahon then characterizes his son as a coward and "the laughing joke of every woman where four baronies meet." In an effort to save Christy, the widow tells Mahon that he has "gone over the hills to catch a steamer."

After Mahon leaves, Christy comes out of hiding and admits that he had mistakenly thought he had killed his father. When he expresses the desire to finish the job, the widow is shocked. She later tells him that the two of them are alike and so proposes that they marry. Christy, however, reaffirms his love for Pegeen. After exacting a promise from Christy that when he marries Pegeen, he will supply her with provisions from the pub, the widow agrees to keep his secret.

Act 3

Later that day, Jimmy and Philly arrive at the pub, discussing Christy's mastery of the village's games and sports and his new role as "playboy of the western world." Soon, Mahon arrives, and the widow tries to convince Jimmy and Philly that Mahon is a raving lunatic and not to pay attention to him. But, as Mahon tells his story, the two men become convinced of its veracity, and they point Christy out to him. After just having won all the day's trophies, Christy tells Pegeen of his love for her in poetic terms, and Pegeen returns his devotion. After some disagreement, Christy convinces Michael that Pegeen should marry him and not Shawn.

When the three return to the pub, Mahon confronts Christy and begins to beat him. Initially, Christy denies that Mahon is his father, but the crowd, along with Pegeen, soon turns against him. When Pegeen calls him "an ugly liar," he threatens to finish the job he had started and goes after his father with a club. The crowd thinks he has really killed him this time and so calls for him to be hanged. After they bind him, Pegeen burns his leg.

When his father appears at the door and sees what the crowd has done to his son, Mahon tells Christy to turn his back on the "villainy of Mayo and the fools is here." The two depart, Christy confidently swaggering out the door. When Shawn insists that he and Pegeen can now marry, Pegeen boxes his ear and laments, "Oh my grief, I've lost him surely. I've lost the only playboy of the western world."

Characters

Jimmy Farrell

Jimmy is a forty-five-year-old "amorous" villager who flatters Pegeen when he visits the pub. He and his friend Philly represent the voice of the villagers as they respond to Christy's story. Jimmy's praise of his actions helps build Christy's confidence and create his mythic stature in the community.

Michael James Flaherty

A jovial publican, the good-humored Michael James allows his daughter to run the pub with a strong hand. Like the other villagers, Michael James initially regards Christy as a hero, but as soon as the truth is discovered, he is one of the first to call for his hanging.

Pegeen Flaherty

Pegeen, a young, attractive woman of twenty, runs the pub for her father. Though Pegeen complains bitterly about being left alone at night, her strength of character and quick tongue suggest she is capable of taking good care of herself. At the beginning of the play, Pegeen is engaged to Shawn, whom she is easily able to control. Pegeen's fiery nature emerges in her dealings with her fiancé, her father, and the Widow Quin, her rival for the attentions of the local men and Christy when he arrives.

Although independent and self-confident, Pegeen allows herself to be seduced by Christy's mythology. Her penchant for romance and her active imagination cause Pegeen to encourage his poetic lovemaking and, as a result, she pledges herself to him. Her lack of clear-sightedness, coupled with her fiery temper, makes Pegeen turn against him when she discovers that he has not killed his father. By the end of the play, however, Pegeen regrets her impulsive actions and laments, "Oh my grief, I've lost him surely. I've lost the only playboy of the western world."

Shawn Keogh

Shawn is engaged to Pegeen at the beginning of the play, although she appears not to think too highly of him. She often calls him Shaneen, which translates to "little Shawn," teasing him for his timid demeanor. Shawn reveals his conservative nature when he declares that he cannot marry Pegeen until he gets approval from the Catholic Church, since the two of them are cousins. This conservatism also causes Shawn to be afraid to be alone with Pegeen, assuming that if word got back to the clergy, they would disapprove. Shawn also shows himself to be a coward when he finds Christy outside the pub, "groaning wicked like a maddening dog," and he is too afraid to get close enough to him to offer aid.

After Christy arrives, Pegeen compares Shawn unfavorably to "the playboy of the western world." Shawn does show some spunk, however, when he tries to bribe Christy into leaving the village with a new suit of clothes and a ticket to America. Yet, when Christy refuses, Shawn resorts to his true self when he admits to the widow that he is too afraid to turn Christy in to the police for fear of retribution.

Christy Mahon

When Christy first comes to Michael James's pub, he is quite fearful about his reception there and being caught by the police. He had just committed a desperate and impulsive act from which he had run in panic, not checking to see if his father was truly dead. Yet, Christy's attempted murder of his father also reveals his rebellious nature. Christy's father had tried to force him to marry the Widow Casey, who is twice his age, blind in one eye, and noted for "misbehavior with the old and young."

Media Adaptations

- *Playboy of the Western World* was adapted for television in 1946 by the BBC and in 1983 in Ireland.

- A film version of *Playboy of the Western World* was produced in Ireland in 1962, starring Siobhan McKenna and Gary Raymond and directed by Brian Hurst.

When Christy first arrives at the pub, Pegeen calls him a "soft lad," but after she hears his story, she determines him to be a hero. When Michael James decides to entrust Pegeen's safety to him while she works alone in the pub at night, Christy becomes more confident in his abilities. His fears soon return, however, when Pegeen, angry at the attention Christy receives from the local girls, suggests that the police might find him out.

After all in the village declare his bravery and embrace him as "the playboy of the western world," Christy swells with pride, believing and becoming his own myth. Since the villagers believe Christy to be a clever, daring man and so expect him to win at all the local sporting events, he becomes the day's hero. Since Pegeen regards Christy as a desirable lover, he becomes passionate and eloquent as he woos her. By the end of the play, Christy retains his newfound strength and courage as he confronts his father and the angry villagers. As a result, Christy's father gains a new respect for him as the two turn their back on the community that rejected him.

Old Mahon

Christy's bad-tempered father has alienated all of his children with his brutish behavior. His constant berating of Christy provoked his initially mild-mannered son to crack his skull. When Old Mahon comes looking for Christy at Michael James's pub, he is bent on revenge. However, when Christy is ill treated by the villagers, Old Mahon's paternal instincts surface as he declares they will turn their backs on "the villainy of Mayo and the fools is here." After Christy stands up to him and threatens to finish the job he had started, Old Mahon gains new respect for his son and follows him out of the village, smiling at his newfound courage.

Pegeen Mike

See Pegeen Flaherty

Philly O'Cullen

Philly, along with Jimmy, represents the collective voice of the townspeople. Whereas Jimmy is more trusting, Philly is more cynical; yet he too is taken in by the excitement surrounding Christy's actions, at least initially. When he learns the truth, he, like the others, is ready to hang the boy.

Widow Quin

The thirty-year-old Widow Quin is a lusty woman who appears to be engaged in a sexual rivalry with Pegeen. The Widow Quin appreciates men, although she hit her husband with a rusty pick, under circumstances never revealed, and as a result he died. This act prompts her to feel an affinity toward Christy, along with the fact that she finds him as attractive as does Pegeen. The Widow Quin is more realistic than her neighbors are, however. She is the first to discover that Christy did not kill his father and immediately strikes a deal with the boy, which would benefit both of them.

Social Conventions

Although there are a few independent characters in the play, like the Widow Quin and Pegeen when she challenges male authority, most act according to social conventions. Shawn Keogh is the most conservative member of the community, refusing to step outside the boundaries set by the Catholic Church. He will not marry Pegeen until he has permission from the Vatican to do so, and he even refuses to be alone with her in fear of the Church's disapproval. Although most in the community consider Shawn's conservatism a mark of cowardice, they follow certain social standards as well. All consider Christy a hero since their community considers this type of rebellion praiseworthy.

Synge illustrates their devotion to convention by sending groups of people to listen to and approve of Christy's story. First, two local men, Jimmy Farrell and Philly O'Cullen, arrive and soon champion him for his bravery. Later, a group of young women appear bearing presents as rewards for his heroic deed. Yet, when the myth is exploded, they all again act according to a herd mentality as they almost lynch Christy, determined that his crimes deserve such harsh treatment.

Rebellion

The play contains an ironic mixture of rebellion and conformity to social conventions. All of the characters, save Shawn, value a rebellious spirit. Pegeen often rebels against convention when she stands up to her father and any other man or woman who comes into the pub. She is not afraid to ignore Church doctrine and derides Shawn for his devotion to it.

The village lionizes Christy for his murderous act because of the nature of that act. By killing his father, Christy was striking a blow against the tyranny of the older generation and of the traditions of the past. As a result, the community applauds his courage as expressed by Jimmy who notes, "bravery's a treasure in a lonesome place, and a lad would kill his father, I'm thinking, could face a foxy divil with a pitchpike on the flags of hell." Ironically, though, when they face the reality of the act as Christy goes after his father with a club outside of the pub, they declare him barbaric and roundly condemn him.

The issues of conformity and rebellion were at the forefront of Irish politics when the play was produced. During the first two decades of the twentieth century, Ireland was in the midst of clashes between those who wanted to maintain the status quo by remaining a colony of England and those who pressed for home rule. The battle between these warring groups was waged throughout the twentieth century and resulted in

Ireland declaring itself a free republic while Northern Ireland retained its colonial status. Clashes, however, still occur in Northern Ireland over the issue of home rule.

Style

Realism and Poetry

The play is an interesting mixture of realism and poetry. Synge's time on the Aran Islands studying the inhabitants helped him create vivid and accurate portraits of Irish life. He writes in his preface to the play that his experiences on the islands provided him "more aid than any learning could have given [him]."

His focus in the play also reflects the dominant themes of realism, with its attention to ordinary people confronting difficult social problems. In *The Playboy of the Western World*, Synge adopts this focus in his depiction of the villagers' treatment of Christy, which is based on a combination of the community's devotion to mythmaking and its mob mentality.

The language of the play is a complex combination of realism and poetry. Dubliners were initially shocked by terms like "shift," referring to women's garments that they found filthy—terms that are considered examples of local color today. When this language is expressed through the unique phrasing and rhythms of the Irish tongue, Synge creates poetry within his prose. Christy's declarations of love to Pegeen are especially praised for their lyric beauty.

Symbolism

As an extension of the theme of mythmaking, Synge transforms Christy into a symbol of the Christ figure. His name adds just a *y,* and, like Christ, he is the son of Mahon (man). The villagers' treatment of him echoes Christ's, as the community first praises and then betrays them both. Ultimately, both are also saved by their fathers.

Topics for Further Study

- Research the movement for home rule in Ireland during the early part of the twentieth century. Explain how the clash between those loyal to England and those who supported Ireland's separation from the British is reflected in the themes of the play.

- During the first few decades of the twentieth century, a "New Woman" emerged who rejected the stereotyped roles of the past and demanded equal rights. Investigate whether this movement also appeared in Ireland. Then, analyze Synge's treatment of women in the play. Do they fit stereotypes, or are they reflective of more modern ideas concerning a woman's place?

- Read Synge's *Riders to the Sea*. Analyze the qualities of Irish life and character as depicted in the play and compare this portrait to that of *The Playboy of the Western World*.

- Think about how an American version of the play would be produced. Would the play be able to retain its main themes, or would they have to be tailored to reflect the American character? Write up a scene-by-scene outline of a possible American version.

Birth of the Irish Theater

At the end of the nineteenth century, Irish writers were divided between two impulses: to express the nostalgia of the heroic legends of the past and to illustrate the beliefs and struggle of the home-rule movement. They met in Dublin, as that city's theater became an artistic representation of Irish country life and legends as well as the politics of the age.

In the 1890s, the Irish middle and upper classes clamored for literature that reflected the nationalistic spirit of the age. They turned their interest to the tales of Ireland's heroic past, recorded by folklorists like Douglas Hyde who studied the Irish language still spoken by the inhabitants of the western coast of the island. William Butler Yeats, who had already established himself as an important Irish poet, discovered the store of poetic material in the stories of this part of the country. Yeats, along with Lady Gregory and Edward Martyn, founded the influential Irish Literary Theatre in 1899 to promote a national movement of the arts. When Martyn, an Ibsen devotee, later left, the remaining members retitled themselves the Abbey Theatre Company. Yeats had envisioned a people's theater where writers and actors could return to the sources of their art: the native speech, habits, and rich mythology of the Irish. Later, Synge would become one of the Abbey's directors.

The first performance at the Irish Literary Theatre was a production of Yeats's *The Countess Cathleen,* on May 8, 1899. Yeats's forte, however, was lyric poetry, not realistic drama. His early verse dramas contained beautiful language but had little dramatic spark. Though he inspired the resurgence of the Irish literary movement, Yeats turned over the literary duties to Lady Gregory, who would pen several plays for the group, and Synge, who became the Abbey's most famous and controversial playwright.

Compare & Contrast

- **Beginning of the 1900s:** In the latter part of the nineteenth century, realism becomes the dominant literary movement in the Western world. In the last decade of the century, symbolism and naturalism emerge as important new movements.

  Today: Musicals like *The Producers* and realitybased plays like *Proof* dominate Broadway.

- **Beginning of the 1900s:** In 1905, Arthur Griffith founded Sinn Fein among Irish Catholics to help establish home rule in Ireland. Demonstrations, especially in

Northern Ireland, often turned violent as England fought to retain control over her colony.

Today: The troubles in Ireland have calmed but have not been resolved. Northern Ireland is still under British rule and as a result, violent skirmishes between the Nationalists and those loyal to England still occur.

- **Beginning of the 1900s:** Samuel Clemens dubbed this era "The Guilded Age," due in large part to the industrialization of the West. During this period, a handful of large industries gained control of the economy in the United States. Those industrialists who profited saw their fortunes grow at a rapid rate while the working class suffered with low wages and dangerous working conditions.

  Today: Public awareness of major companies exploiting foreign workers has grown. Many fear that the current push for economic globalization will reinforce the imbalances between the rich and the poor.

Realism

In the late nineteenth century, playwrights turned away from what they considered the artificiality of melodrama to focus on the commonplace in the context of everyday contemporary life. They rejected the flat characterizations and unmotivated violent action typical of melodrama. Their work, along with much of the experimental fiction written during that period, adopts the tenets of realism, a new literary movement that took a serious look at believable characters and their sometimes problematic interactions with society. To accomplish this goal, realistic drama focuses on the commonplace and eliminates the unlikely coincidences and excessive emotionalism of melodrama. Dramatists like Henrik Ibsen discard traditional sentimental theatrical forms as they chronicle the strengths and weaknesses of ordinary people confronting difficult social problems, like the restrictive conventions under which nineteenth-century women suffered. Writers who embraced realism use settings and props that reflect their characters' daily lives and realistic dialogue that replicates natural speech patterns.

Synge adopted many of the characteristics of realism in his plays but also added poetic elements. As a result, his plays became a complex mixture of traditional forms arranged in new ways. Ann Saddlemyer writes, in her introduction to Oxford's collection of Synge's plays, that Synge's study of the inhabitants of the Aran Islands resulted in an "appreciation of their heightened sensitivity to the changing moods of nature and the harsh conditions they endured," which helped him develop "his own aesthetic, a blending of romantic pantheism and ironic realism." Synge writes in his preface to *The Playboy of the Western World* that he rejected the realism of Ibsen and Zola whom he argued "dealt with the reality of life in joyless and pallid words." He insisted that "on the stage one must have reality, and one must have joy … the rich joy found only in what is superb and wild in reality."

Critical Overview

Irish theater had never experienced such a violent audience response as it did when *The Playboy of the Western World* premiered on January 26, 1907. Theatergoers loudly proclaimed their disapproval of the plot, which appeared to glorify parricide; of what they considered offensive dialogue; and of Synge's depiction of the Irish character. Hisses continually disrupted the performances during the play's first week, and arrests were made nightly. The most controversial line in the play was Christy's declaration that he was not interested in "a drift of chosen females, standing in their shifts itself." Similar outbursts occurred during a 1909 revival of the play and during performances in North America in 1911. County Clare, County Kerry, and Liverpool issued official condemnations of the play. Elizabeth Coxhead, in her article on Synge for *British Writers,* explains that when the play was produced, "Irish nationalistic feelings were high, and Synge's plays had caused offense before among those who felt that Ireland and the Irish should always be depicted with decorum on the stage."

While the January 28 edition of the *Irish Times* would observe that the play's language brought "what in other respects was a brilliant success to an inglorious conclusion," most reviews roundly condemned it. The *Freeman's Journal* considered the "squalid, offensive production" to be an "unmitigated, protracted libel upon Irish peasant men and worse still upon peasant girlhood," citing its "barbarous jargon" and "the elaborate and incessant cursings of [the] repulsive creatures" in the play.

The riots during the first week's performances prompted Yeats, a firm supporter of the play, to hold a public debate on the issue of artistic freedom. Susan Stone-Blackburn, in her article on Synge in the *Dictionary of Literary Biography,* quotes Yeats's argument that "every man has a right to hear" a play "and condemn it if he pleases, but no man has a right to interfere with another man hearing a play and judging for himself." In an effort to instill a sense of national pride, he insisted, "The country that condescends either to bully or to permit itself to be bullied soon ceases to have any fine qualities."

The play's reputation has grown throughout the twentieth century to the point that it is now recognized as Synge's masterwork. P. P. Howe, in his critical study of Synge, insisted that *The Playboy of the Western World* "brought to the contemporary stage the most rich and copious store of character since Shakespeare." Charles A. Bennett, in his essay "The Plays of John M. Synge," considered it to be Synge's "most characteristic work. It is riotous with the quick rush of life, a tempest of the passions with the glare of laughter at its heart." Norman Podhoretz, in his assessment of the play in *Twentieth Century Interpretations of "The Playboy of the Western World": A Collection of Critical Essays,* championed it as "a dramatic masterpiece" that expresses "the undeveloped poet coming to consciousness of himself as man and as artist."

What Do I Read Next?

- In *The Abbey Theatre* (1987), E. H. Mikhail presents a comprehensive history of the Abbey Theatre from the beginning to the present time, focusing on the actors, playwrights, directors, and supporters of the theater.

- Following Yeats's suggestion, Synge lived for a time on the Aran Islands, where he made careful observations of the inhabitants there. He gathered together his notes in essay form, which were eventually published as *The Aran Islands* (1907).

- *Riders to the Sea* was produced by the Irish National Theatre Society in Dublin in 1904. Like *Playboy of the Western World,* this play presents a realistic yet poetic vision of Irish life, specifically on one of the Aran Islands off the western coast of Ireland.

- *In the Shadow of the Glen* (1903) was Synge's first play to be produced by the Irish National Theatre Society in Dublin in 1904. It began the author's battle with Irish theater patrons over his authentic portrait of Irish life.

Sources

Bennett, Charles A., "The Plays of J. M. Synge," in the *Yale Review,* January 1912.

Corkery, Daniel, *Synge and Anglo-Irish Literature,* Mercier, 1931.

Coxhead, Elizabeth, "J. M. Synge / Lady Augusta Gregory," in *British Writers,* Vol. 6, 1983, pp. 307–18.

Howe, P. P., *J. M. Synge: A Critical Study,* Martin Secker, 1912.

Podhoretz, Norman, "Synge's *Playboy:* Morality and the Hero," in *Twentieth Century Interpretations of "The Playboy of the Western World": A Collection of Critical Essays,* Prentice-Hall, 1969.

Review of *The Playboy of the Western World,* in *Freeman's Journal,* January 28, 1907.

Review of *The Playboy of the Western World,* in *Irish Times,* January 28, 1907.

Saddlemyer, Ann, "Introduction," in *Playboy of the Western World and Other Plays,* Oxford University Press, 1998, pp. vii–xxi.

Skelton, Robin, *The Writings of J. M. Synge,* Thames & Hudson, 1971.

Stone-Blackburn, Susan, "John Millington Synge," in *Dictionary of Literary Biography,* Vol. 10, Pt. 2, *Modern British Dramatists 1900–1945: M–Z,* edited by Stanley Weintraub, Gale Research, 1982, pp. 168–84.

Synge, J. M., "Preface to *Playboy of the Western World*," in *The Playboy of the Western World and Other Plays,* Oxford University Press, 1998, pp. 96–97.

Yeats, William Butler, "Preface to *The Well of the Saints,*" in *The Playboy of the Western World and Other Plays,* Oxford University Press, 1998, pp. 52–56.

Further Reading

Bushrui, S. B., ed., *Sunshine and the Moon's Delight,* Colin Smythe, 1972.

> Bushrui edits several essays on Synge's plays, including several on his use of language.

Greene, David H., and Edward M. Stephens, *J. M. Synge, 1871–1909,* rev. ed., Macmillan, 1989.

> This indispensable biography contains little criticism of the works, but it offers a wealth of information about Synge's life and influences on his work.

Price, Alan, *Synge and Anglo-Irish Drama,* Methuen, 1961.

> Price presents insightful analyses of Synge's plays and places them in a literary historical context.

Skelton, Robin, *J. M. Synge and His World,* Viking, 1971.

> Skelton's admirable work provides commentary on Synge's life as well as relevant historical background.

Lightning Source UK Ltd.
Milton Keynes UK
UKHW020815270819
348683UK00017B/844/P

9 781375 392945